Where to find minibeasts

On a plant

Sarah Ridley

W
FRANKLIN WATTS
LONDON•SYDNEY

Franklin Watts Australia,
Level 17/207 Kent Street,
Sydney, NSW 2000

Series editor: Sarah Peutrill
Art director: Jonathan Hair
Design: Jane Hawkins
Illustrations: John Alston

Dewey number: 595.7
ISBN: 978 1 4451 0274 0

Printed in China

Franklin Watts is a division of
Hachette Children's Books,
an Hachette UK company.
www.hachette.co.uk

The measures for the minibeasts in this book are typical sizes for the type of species shown in the photograph. Different species vary in size enormously however.

Picture credits and species guide:
Front cover top: Boy inspecting insect, Jim Sugar/Corbis. **Front cover below:** Monarch butterfly (*Danaus plexippus*), Arvind Balaraman/Shutterstock. **2:** Seven Spot Ladybird (*Coccinella septempunctata*), Christian Musat/Shutterstock. **3:** Honey bee (*Apis mellifera*), Richard Seymour/Shutterstock. **6:** Marbled White (*Melanargia galathea*) and Large Garden Bee (*Bombus ruderatus*) on Pyramidal orchid (*Anacamptis pyramidalis*), Bernd Zoller/Imagebroker/FLPA Images. **7l:** Honey bee (*Apis mellifera*) approaching flower, Adam Tinney/Shutterstock. **7tr:** Cinnebar moth caterpillars (*Tyria jacobaeæ*) feeding on Ragwort (Senecio jacobaea), Jan Vanmeer/Foto Natura/FLPA Images. **8t:** Monarch butterfly (*Danaus plexippus*), Arvind Balaraman/Shutterstock. **8br:** Peacocks (*Inachis io*) & Small Tortoiseshells (*Aglais urticae*) butterflies on buddleia, Stephen Dalton/NHPA. **9t:** Honey bee (*Apis mellifera*) cells, Florin Tirlea/Shutterstock. **9b:** Hoverfly (*Syrphus ribesii*), Gertjan Hooijer/Shutterstock. **10:** Honey bee (Apis mellifera) collecting pollen, Douglas Adams/Shutterstock. **11bl:** Crab Spider (*Misumena vatia*) feeding on Bumblebee (*Bombus lucorum*) on Betony flower (*Stachys officinalis*), Phil McLean/FLPA Images. **11tr:** Honey bee (*Apis mellifera*), Richard Seymour/Shutterstock. **12t:** Monarch caterpillar (*Danaus plexippus*) eating a Milkweed leaf (*Asclepias syriaca*), Ed Reschke/Still Pictures. **12b:** Green Shield bug (*Palomena prasina*), Dariusz /Shutterstock. **13t:** Monarch caterpillar (*Danaus plexippus*) on a milkweed plant (*Asclepias, syriaca*), Gilles De Cruyenaere/Shutterstock. **13b:** Boy inspecting insect, Jim Sugar/Corbis. **14t:** Drone fly (*Eristalis tenax*) on leaf, Ismael Montero Verdu/Shutterstock. **14b:** Seven-spot ladybird beetles (*Coccinella septempunctata*) hibernating, Dr Jeremy Burgess/SPL. **15t:** Whitethroat (*Sylvia communis*), Rick Thornton/Shutterstock. **15c:** Large White Butterfly eggs (*Pieris brassicae*), George Bernard/NHPA. **15b:** Small Tortoiseshell Butterfly (*Aglais urticae*) - female laying eggs on stinging nettle (*Urtica dioica*), Michael Maconachie/Ecoscene. **16l:** Seven spot ladybird (*Coccinella septempunctata*), Christian Musat/Shutterstock. **16tr:** Black Bean aphids (*Aphis fabae*), Ernie James/NHPA. **16b:** Ladybird row - native & invasive species, from left to right - Seven-Spot (*Coccinella septempunctata*), Harlequin (*Harmonia axyridis*), Harlequin, Two-Spot (*Adalia bipunctata*), Fourteen-Spot (*Propylea quatuordecimpunctata*), Mark Bowler/NHPA. **17t:** Honeypot Ants (*Myrmecocystus*) tending black aphids (*Aphis fabae*),pixelman/Shutterstock. **17b:** Seven spot ladybird (*Coccinella septempunctata*) & black ant (*Lasius niger*), Christophe Ratier/NHPA. **18t:** Wartbiter, female (*Decticus verrucivorus*), Martin Lindler/NHPA. **18b:** Common Green Grasshopper (*Omocestus viridulus*),Luká Hejtman/Shutterstock. **19t:** Froghopper secretion, Cuckpoo Spit (*Philaenus spumarius*), froghopper froth, Laurie Campbell/NHPA. **19cl:** Common froghopper (*Philaenus spumarius*) nymph with cuckoo spit on rose stem, Nigel Cattlin/FLPA Images. **19b:** Froghopper (*Philaenus spumarius*) next to white froth 'cuckoo spit'. Philippe Clement/Nature PL. **20-21:** Spider's web, Marika Eglite/Shutterstock. **21:** Banded garden spider (*Argiope trifasciata*) and prey, adv/Shutterstock. **22:** Polyphemus moth (*Antheraea polyphemus*) on flower, David Kelly/Shutterstock. **23t:** Peaches, Gerrit de Vries/Shutterstock. **23bl:** Tulip-tree Beauty Moth, (*Epimecis hortaria*), Michael Pettigrew/Shutterstock. **23cr:** Brown cane sugar, Paul Paladin/Shutterstock. **23c:** Plastic container, Timothy Geiss /Shutterstock. **23br:** Torch, Nataliya Hora/Shutterstock. **24t:** Plastic boxes, Scott Rothstein/Shutterstock. **24c:** Magnifying glass Shutterstock. **24cb:** Paintbrush, Adam Borkowski/Shutterstock. **24b:** Boy, Watts. **25t:** Seven-spot ladybird (*Coccinella septempunctata*), Steve Shoup/Shutterstock. **25b:** Girl drawing, Photocreate/Shutterstock. **31:** Honey bee (*Apis mellifera*), Douglas Adams/Shutterstock

Contents

Words in **bold** are in the glossary on pages 28–29.

Minibeasts and plants

Plants are great places to find minibeasts. Plants provide minibeasts with shelter, safety, food – or all three. Plants can be somewhere to lay their eggs or rear their young.

What is a minibeast?

Minibeast is the name given to thousands of small animals. Although many are **insects**, others are not. Minibeasts do not have **backbones** so scientists call them **invertebrates**.

▲ Bees and butterflies are just two types of minibeast that visit flowers in search of food.

Minibeast habitats

Minibeasts can be found on plants that grow in all sorts of **habitats**, from deserts to forests. A habitat is the place where certain plants and animals like to live. Habitats can be small, such as a garden or plant, or huge, like a desert.

▶ Cinnabar moths lay their eggs on ragwort plants, which their caterpillars love to eat.

This caterpillar is 3 cm long.

Plants need minibeasts

Minibeasts help plants to make new **seeds**, which will grow into new plants. When a minibeast flies from flower to flower, **pollen** from the flower sticks to the minibeast. Some of this pollen rubs off when the minibeast touches another flower, allowing the flower to make seeds.

This bee is 2 cm long.

▲ This bee is carrying pollen on its furry body and hairy legs.

TOP TIP!

It isn't always easy to spot minibeasts on plants, but you can learn how to look – watch out for the top tips in this book.

Flower power

Flowering plants attract flying minibeasts that are searching for food. Inside each flower is a sweet liquid called **nectar**. This is the minibeasts' food.

▲ The butterfly's long tube-like mouth reaches inside the flower to suck up nectar.

This butterfly has a wingspan of 7 cm.

TOP TIP!

If you want to attract more butterflies, ask your parents or school to plant a honeysuckle, buddleia or lavender plant. Good gardening websites have other suggestions, some of which can be grown in a window box or flowerpot.

▲ The strong smell of buddleia flowers attracts butterflies.

Bees and nectar

Bees also visit flowers for their nectar. They suck it up and store it in their special 'honey stomach'. Back at the **hive** or nest, bees use the nectar to make honey.

▶ Bees store honey in honeycombs. They eat honey themselves and feed it to their young.

This hoverfly is 1.5 cm long.

Look out for hoverflies feeding on nectar. They are actually harmless flies but they look like wasps, so **predators** think they have a nasty sting.

Plants need visitors

While they are searching for nectar, minibeasts such as bees, beetles, butterflies and hoverflies pick up pollen from the flowers they visit.

Pollen

Pollen is a powder made by a plant's flowers. Some pollen sticks to the minibeasts' legs or the hairs on their body and then rubs off onto another flower. This **pollinates** the flower, allowing it to make seeds.

▲ Bees also collect some pollen in tiny sacs on their back legs. Back at the hive or nest, they feed the pollen to baby bees, called **larvae**.

Bees are special

Bees pollinate more flowers than any other kind of minibeast. Pollination allows the plant to make **fruits** and seeds, which grow into new plants.

Although pollen is also carried on the wind, without bees many farmers and gardeners would be unable to grow the fruit, vegetables and seeds that we eat every day.

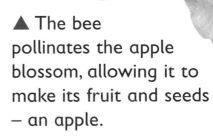

▲ The bee pollinates the apple blossom, allowing it to make its fruit and seeds – an apple.

TOP TIP!

Some minibeast predators wait on flowers to grab an unsuspecting minibeast as it lands. Look out for spiders, for example, eating other minibeasts!

◀ This spider has caught a bee as it visits a flower for food.

Look at a leaf

This caterpillar is 5 cm long.

While some minibeasts visit flowers, other minibeasts prefer leaves.

TOP TIP!

If you can see that a plant leaf has been nibbled, look carefully to see if the animal that did it is still around.

▲ Caterpillars have strong jaws for eating leaves.

Resting and eating

Sometimes minibeasts use leaves as a safe resting place, or as a good spot to sunbathe. Many minibeasts feed on plant leaves. Caterpillars eat leaves, while some **bugs**, such as shield bugs, suck out the juice.

This shield bug is 1.5 cm long.

◄ This shield bug is the same colour as the leaves it sits on so predators find it hard to spot. Other types of shield bug can be brightly coloured.

Keeping caterpillars

If you want to watch caterpillars closely, you could keep them in a plastic box for a few days.

You will need:

• A small plastic box, such as a margarine tub

• Leaves of a plant with caterpillars on it

• A magnifying glass

• A small paintbrush, in case you need to move the caterpillars

What to do:

• Make sure the plastic box is clean and dry.

• Move your caterpillars into their new home along with some of the plant that they are eating.

• Watch them munching. You can use the magnifying glass to see them better.

• Remember to place a lid with small holes in it on the box when you want a rest, otherwise the caterpillars won't be there when you return!

• Give the caterpillars fresh leaves and, after a few days, return them to the plant where you found them.

Under a leaf

Carefully turn over a leaf to see if any minibeasts are sheltering from the sun, the rain or from predators. You might find butterflies, ladybirds, flies or caterpillars.

▲ The leaf provides shade and safety for this fly.

Ladybirds are about 0.6 cm long. ├─┤

A winter home

Sometimes ladybirds gather under a leaf in the autumn to sleep through the winter. This is called **hibernation**.

◀ When ladybirds hibernate, they try to keep warm by sleeping close together.

TOP TIP!

Minibeasts are the favourite food of some birds, toads, hedgehogs and other animals. As a result, minibeasts often hide themselves on plants. Remember to search for them all over the plant.

Butterfly eggs

You may find tiny dots of colour under a leaf. These are butterfly eggs. The butterfly lays eggs on the plants that its caterpillars like eating.

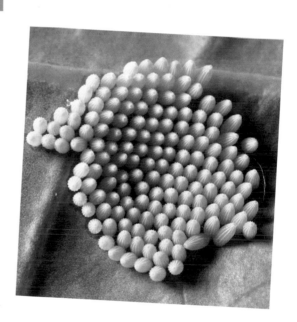

▲ If you find butterfly eggs, keep checking the plant. One day they will hatch into tiny caterpillars. This photo is much bigger than real life.

◄ Watch closely if you see a butterfly curve its body under a leaf like this. This is how a butterfly lays its eggs.

Sucking at stems

Sometimes plant **stems** and leaves become covered in tiny minibeasts called aphids. They are all feeding on the plant, sucking out its juices, called **sap.**

▶ These aphids are black, but others are green.

An aphid is about 2 mm long. ▬

Ladybirds love aphids

If you look carefully, you may see ladybirds eating aphids. Aphids damage plants, so ladybirds are a gardener's friend.

There are many different types of ladybird, and not all of them are red. Some are yellow or even black, and they have different numbers of spots.

◀ A ladybird can eat a hundred aphids a day.

This ant is 1 cm long.

Ants love aphids, too

Sometimes you will see ants with aphids, but ants don't eat aphids. Ants like to 'milk' aphids for a sweet liquid they make called **honeydew**. They collect the honeydew and feed it to their young.

▲ Ants look after aphids so they can collect their honeydew.

Ant attack!

If you see ants, ladybirds and aphids together, the ants may be attacking the ladybirds to try to make them go away.

◀ This ant is trying to protect aphids from their ladybird enemy.

Clinging to stems

The stem of a plant provides another safe place for minibeasts to rest, eat or even make their home.

Crickets and grasshoppers

Tall grasses attract crickets and grasshoppers. They eat plants and use them as a hiding place. Crickets and grasshoppers can be difficult to spot but listen out for their chirping noise in the summer.

▶ The cricket has long **antennae**.

This cricket is about 1.5 cm long.

The grasshopper rubs its back leg against its wing to make a chirping noise. The cricket makes a similar noise by rubbing its wings together. They do it to find mates, and to tell others to keep away from their patch.

This grasshopper is about 1.7 cm long.

▶ The grasshopper has short, thick antennae.

◀ ▲ The froth creates a safe home in which the young froghopper can feed and grow until it turns into an adult. ▶

This froghopper is about 0.6 cm long.
⊢⊣

Froghopper froth

In spring you may find some froth on plant stems. Some people call it 'cuckoo spit'. If you look closely you will see something dark moving inside. This is a froghopper larva, also called a **nymph**. The larva makes the froth from plant sap and air and blows it out of its bottom.

19

Wonderful webs

Some minibeasts don't feed on plants at all, but use plants to help them catch food. Spiders often attach their webs to plants.

TOP TIP!

Look out for webs like this early in the morning or after rain or frost, when tiny drops of water cling to the web like diamonds.

Death traps

Unsuspecting minibeasts land on or fly into a spider's web and become trapped. The spider hurries over, injects the minibeast with poison, then either sucks out its blood or wraps it up and stores it for later.

▶ This spider has spun a silk bag around its **prey**.

A spider spins a **web** using its **spinnerets**. The spinnerets produce a strong, fine, silk. There are around 30 metres of silk in each garden spider's web.

Plants in the evening

While many minibeasts are active during the day, others come to life in the evening and the night.

This moth has a wingspan of 15 cm.

Moths

Some moths fly in the daytime, but many search for plant nectar in the evening. Their favourite plants include honeysuckle, evening primrose and night-scented stock. All of these plants produce a strong scent, or smell. Moths use their antennae to follow this scent.

▲ Moths find flower nectar by following the flower's scent.

 Moths are very similar to butterflies. One big difference is that moths usually rest with their wings out flat, rather than closed together like most butterflies.

Attracting moths

If you don't have any of the moths' favourite plants in your garden at home or at school, you can try to attract some moths by using this sugary paint.

You will need:
- Mashed ripe fruit
- Warm water
- A bowl and fork
- Brown sugar
- A paintbrush
- A torch

What to do:
- Ask an adult to help you mix up a sweet liquid made from mashed ripe fruit, brown sugar and warm water.

- Paint the mixture onto a tree trunk or even onto a wooden fence.

- Wait until evening and use a torch to help you see the feeding moths.

This moth has a wingspan of 5 cm.

◄ Can you spot the moth resting on this tree trunk?

Big minibeast hunt

Discover how many minibeasts are in a bush or a tree by following these instructions.

You will need:

• A big white bed sheet, or a large piece of white paper

• A magnifying glass

• Plastic containers for collecting minibeasts

• A small paintbrush for gently moving minibeasts about

What to do:

• Choose a bush or a tree and place the sheet or paper underneath it. Give the plant a good shake.

▶ Shake the bush or tree only once or twice or you may hurt the minibeasts.

- If you are lucky, lots of tiny creatures will fall down onto your sheet or paper.

- You have to be very gentle with minibeasts as they are small animals that can easily be hurt. Use the paintbrush or a piece of grass or twig to move them.

- Carefully place some of the minibeasts in your containers for a closer look.

- Use the identification guide on the next pages to work out what you have found.

- Remember to put the minibeasts back up in the branches of the bush or tree.

TOP TIP!

Spring and summer are good seasons to search for minibeasts on plants. Many minibeasts are attracted to plants at this time in search of food.

▶ Sketching minibeasts is a good way to keep a record of what you have seen.

Identification guide

Use this guide to help you identify the minibeasts that you find. They are listed in the order they are first mentioned. Other common minibeasts are listed at the end. As there are thousands of different minibeasts, you may need to use a field guide as well.

Bee: Bees are flying insects and there are many types. Some live in nests with other bees while others live alone. All bees sting if they feel they are in danger, so don't touch!

Fly: There are thousands of different types of fly. They are all flying insects with one pair of wings. Use a field guide to identify the type.

Butterfly: The butterfly is a flying insect. It lays eggs that will hatch into caterpillars. In time, the caterpillars will turn into butterflies.

Beetle: Beetles are insects and they have two pairs of wings. One of these sets of wings are hard to protect the soft set underneath.

Moth: A flying insect, similar to a butterfly and with the same lifecycle. Many moths fly at night, searching for nectar.

Spider: Spiders come in all shapes and sizes but they all have eight legs and a body in two parts. They are **arachnids**.

 **Hoverfly:** Hoverflies look like wasps or bees, to give them protection from predators, but are in fact flies. Note that the hoverfly has only one pair of wings, unlike the bee or the wasp.

Shield bug: An insect that is shaped like an African shield. Shield bugs belong to the bug family and suck sap out of plants.

Wasp: A flying insect with two pairs of wings, unlike the hoverfly that has only one pair. If wasps feel in danger they will sting, so don't touch!

Ladybird: A flying insect with two pairs of wings. Ladybirds are small beetles that eat aphids.

Aphid: A small green or black insect that belongs to the bug family. Like all bugs, it has a sharp, piercing mouth. It feeds by sucking sap out of plants.

Harvestman: A harvestman is not an insect and it is not a spider. It has eight legs and its body is in one part. It is an arachnid, like the spider, and it can run very fast.

Ant: A small, six-legged insect with long antennae. It spends most of its time collecting food and taking it back to its colony – the group of ants it lives with.

Lacewing: This flying insect has almost see-through wings. It feeds mostly on aphids and other small insects.

Cricket: You can tell the cricket from the grasshopper by its long antennae. It is an insect with strong back legs for jumping but also has wings so it can fly.

Damselfly: This flying insect has two pairs of wings and huge eyes. The larva lives in water but the adult flies about feeding on minibeasts.

Grasshopper: An insect with strong back legs for jumping, as well as wings for flying. It has shorter antennae than the cricket.

Dragonfly: This flying insect, very like the damselfly, usually rests with its wings held out, while the damselfly usually folds its wings above its body.

Froghopper: An insect that belongs to the bug family. The common froghopper nymph makes a frothy home for itself to protect it from predators.

Slug: This animal has a soft body and no legs. It belongs to the mollusc family of animals.

Earwig: A small, shiny insect that usually lives in dark, damp places such as cracks in wood or walls, or under a stone.

Snail: The snail carries its shell on its soft body and belongs to the mollusc family, like the slug (above).

Glossary

Antennae The pair or pairs of bendy threads joined to an insect's head and used for smell, taste and touch.

Arachnid An animal with eight legs, like a spider, harvestman or mite.

Backbone The line of bones down the middle of the skeleton.

Bug The name for an insect with piercing mouth parts, which it uses to suck sap from a plant or blood from another animal.

Fruit The fruit contains the seeds of a plant.

Habitat A place where certain plants and animals like to live.

Hibernation Spending the winter in a deep state of sleep.

Hive The home for honeybees, set up by bee-keepers so that they can keep bees and harvest honey.

Honeydew A sweet liquid made by an aphid, squeezed out of its bottom and collected by ants to feed to its young.

Insects A huge group of animals. All insects have a body in three parts – the head at one end, thorax in the middle and abdomen at the other end. Six legs are attached to the thorax and many insects also have wings.

Invertebrates A huge group of animals without a backbone including insects, worms and spiders.

Larva (*plural,* **larvae**)
The stage in the lifecycle of many insects after they hatch from eggs.

Nectar The sweet liquid made by flowers and eaten by many insects.

Nymph A type of larva (see above).

Pollen A fine powder made by the flower of a plant that fertilises other flowers.

Pollination This is when pollen (see above) lands on a flower, allowing it to make fruit and seeds for the plant.

Predators Animals that eat other animals, rather than plants or dead things.

Prey Animals that other animals hunt to eat.

Sap The liquid inside a plant.

Seed The part of a plant from which another plant can grow.

Spinneret The part of the spider that makes silk.

Stem The part of a plant that is above ground and holds the leaves and flowers.

Websites to visit

www.naturegrid.org.uk/grassland/index.html
Try to find all the minibeasts hiding on this site, with lots of information about each animal.

www.buglife.org.uk
Visit the Buglife site for masses of information about minibeasts.

Note to parents and teachers:
Every effort has been made by the Publishers to ensure that these websites are suitable for children, that they are of the highest educational value, and that they contain no inappropriate or offensive material. However, because of the nature of the Internet, it is impossible to guarantee that the contents of these sites will not be altered. We strongly advise that Internet access is supervised by a responsible adult.

Index